Work Freedom

God turns burden into blessing

Brittany Ezell

Copyright © 2022 by Brittany Symone Ezell

ISBN: 979-8-9857392-0-6

All rights reserved. This book or any portion thereof may not be reproduced or used in any manner whatsoever without the express written permission of the publisher except for the use of brief quotations in a book review.

Scripture quotations marked (NLT) are taken from the Holy Bible, New Living Translation, copyright ©1996, 2004, 2015 by Tyndale House Foundation. Used by permission of Tyndale House Publishers, Carol Stream, Illinois 60188. All rights reserved.

Scripture quotations marked (NIV) are taken from the Holy Bible, New International Version®, NIV®. Copyright © 1973, 1978, 1984, 2011 by Biblica, Inc.™ Used by permission of Zondervan. All rights reserved worldwide. www.zondervan.comThe "NIV" and "New International Version" are trademarks registered in the United States Patent and Trademark Office by Biblica, Inc.™

Scripture quotations marked (KJV) are from the King James Version. Public domain.

Scripture quotations marked (AMP) are taken from the Amplified Bible, Copyright © 2015 by The Lockman Foundation. Used by permission.

Scripture quotations marked (AMPCE) are taken from the Amplified Bible, Copyright © 1954, 1958, 1962, 1964, 1965, 1987 by The Lockman Foundation. Used by permission.

Definitions are taken from Google Online Dictionary Powered by Oxford Languages (unless otherwise noted). languages.oup.com/google-dictionary-en/

This book is dedicated to my *Heavenly Father*, my *Lord and Savior Jesus Christ*, and His *Holy Spirit* without whom I could not have written this book or finished the good work that was started in me.

Acknowledgements

Special Thanks to…

God for completely shifting my attitude about work.

My parents - My dad Winfield Ezell, for all of the support you have given me in my highs and lows; thank you for always being there. My mom Doris Virgil, for your continuous prayers over my life; they have availeth much.

My siblings Whitney, Win, Tory, and Tim for being an inspiration to not settle and push forward in reaching my dreams.

My amazing sister in Christ, Alyssa Gordon, who called me every week, shared God's wisdom, and encouraged me to stay the course.

My church family at Believers' Bible Christian Church and all my church homes that laid a foundation over the years, and have been a source of love and support from youth until now - Mount Pleasant Missionary Baptist Church, Wheat Street Baptist Church, Elizabeth Baptist Church, and Evolve Life Church.

My spiritual leaders: Pastors Theo and Octavia McNair, Minister Tim McNair (for sharing your insights), Pastor Mike Owens (for every encouraging word), and Rosa Cohen (my honorary mom in Christ).

Every family member, friend, and co-worker who inspired me to write this book and held me accountable throughout this journey.

Contents

Preface 1
Introduction 5
Chapter 1: Preparing for the Unknown 9
Chapter 2: Difficult Work Environments 17
Chapter 3: Fighting Off Discontentment..................31
Chapter 4: Getting Past Worry & Doubt 39
Chapter 5: Seeking Purpose & Passion.....................51
Chapter 6: Managing Frustration 57
Chapter 7: Focusing on What's Important................65
Chapter 8: Faith + Works is Alive..............................79
Chapter 9: Entrusting God with Work.......................89
Conclusion..99
About the Author...103

Preface

Let's be honest - while some may be blessed to do work they truly love and enjoy, for many, work is merely a means to attain the things we want and desire in life. What happens when we become so focused on the correlation between work and income that our necessity for money leaves us feeling burdened, anxious, fearful, or trapped? We cannot afford to set our dependency of being fulfilled and provided for on the work that we do.

While God does desire for us to be diligent workers at our assignments, He never intended for work to become our source - God is our Source of provision in all things, financial and otherwise. Would you be surprised to know that I went 4 years with little to no work and did not lack a thing - I certainly was!

Work Freedom

And for those who don't know me personally - no, I did not have a spouse at the time (so no additional income there), I am not a trust fund baby, and I did not win the quick pick. However, I do have a Heavenly Daddy Whose children don't have to beg for bread (Psalms 37:25), Who promised He will never leave me or forsake me (Deuteronomy 31:6), Who can literally supply needs from the most unlikely of places (Matthew 17:27; 2 Kings 4:1-7) and saw fit for others to bless me during my hardship (Philippians 4:14).

Now I'm not encouraging anyone to stop working - because I believe that God gives us all assignments to do, even if you aren't working a 9 to 5. You should always work towards the things that God has placed inside of you to do. I just encourage you to not have the false mindset that your job is providing for your needs and wants. God has blessed you with work to do, but even if that work went away, you would still have God, His Love, and your ability to fully depend on Him to make a way. The apostle Paul shared his experience stating, "Not that I was ever in

Preface

need, for I have learned how to be content with whatever I have. I know how to live on almost nothing or with everything. I have learned the secret of living in every situation, whether it is with a full stomach or empty, with plenty or little. For I can do everything through Christ, who gives me strength." Philippians 4:11-13 (NLT)

Introduction

I had to change my mentality about work. It was the only way that I could truly walk in freedom in my life. My hope is that as you read this book, God will reveal areas of your work that you can surrender to Him. No matter what type of work you do, whether it be schoolwork or professional work, physically or mentally strenuous, fast-paced or slow, interesting or boring, time-consuming or flexible - you can walk a lot lighter and easier if you walk with God day-by-day.

If I can be honest with you all, I never really "liked" to work. I was always ambitious because I wanted financial stability, but I had a different long-term vision for my life. I always wanted to be a stay-at-home mom (which I originally didn't view as "work,"); albeit there is a great level of work and effort required to be a stay-at-home mom, I deemed this work as a preference. While my heart still desires to manage my home as a wife and mother, I am grateful that my husband and children did not have to be the testing ground for God to show me the importance of work in and outside of the home.

Instead, it was in the corporate setting and in my pursuits of running my own business that God taught me very valuable lessons about having the right perspective about work. Not just having positive feelings when going to work, but a total mind shift about this extremely important area of life - an area of life that likely consumes most people's days.

You may already love to work; in fact, you may be a workaholic! Or you may fall somewhere in between where I was and desiring to work all the time. Either way, you can benefit from completely letting go of the hold that you have on your work and turning it over to the Original Creator, Boss, and CEO: Our Heavenly Father, God.

Introduction

I pray that by the end of this book:

- You confirm what kind of work God is leading you to do and the purpose of it
- You have peace about every aspect of your work
- Your trust in God goes to new levels that they have never gone before

Chapter 1: Preparing for the Unknown

Each day we face new experiences at work. We may be starting a new job, a new role, a new business, getting a new project or manager, or entering a new fiscal year - whatever your new day at work brings, it is important to prepare for this transition.

How do we best prepare? We prepare by inviting God into our minds, our workplace, and our experience BEFORE we enter our time of work. Preparing for the unknown must start with seeking God first because He is all-knowing.

"You have searched me, LORD, and you know me. You know when I sit and when I rise; you perceive my thoughts from afar. You discern my going out and my lying down; you are familiar with all my ways." Psalms 139:1-3 (NIV)

Work Freedom

God is familiar with all your ways. Which is great because that means He knows where you have been, where you are going, who is going to be there, what you will encounter, and what thoughts will be on your mind while you are there. But God doesn't just know you - He knows every person and every circumstance that you will encounter with your work, so He can give you the insight, wisdom, revelation, and understanding that you need before you step foot into the day and as you go along it.

I used to go into interview situations with fear and trembling - both physically and mentally - because I didn't know what they were going to say, what they were going to expect me to say, how they were going to act, and what the day would be like. However, once I started preparing in advance by seeking God and asking Him to show me what opportunities were for me, to close any doors that weren't beneficial, and to give me wisdom throughout the process - He illuminated what I needed to review and gave me favor with the people that I interacted with.

Preparing for the Unknown

I'm telling you this because God is more than available and wanting to do the same for you. He wants to enter the workplace with you everyday and give you the readiness to be confidently at ease, but you must invite Him. Matthew 6:33 tells us to, "Seek the Kingdom of God above all else, and live righteously, and he will give you everything you need." (NLT) The key part being *above all else*. God has to be and rightfully should be first - the first for us to consult for help, advice, strength, energy, ideas, peace, patience, joy, finances - whatever it is that we are needing or hoping for.

It's not something that always happens overnight - it's a process. As much as we love God and truly do want to satisfy Him and do His will, most are not acclimated or able to come to God before they start their workday. Either they don't allow enough time before they have to get to work, or they think their plans for the start of the day is more essential than taking the time to align with Him. Of course, we don't like to think that we are not prioritizing God, but if we seek

Him first I promise that He will help you do everything else you need to!

You may be saying to yourself that you aren't starting anything new - and if you are thinking along those lines - I would like to offer up that every moment we have here on this earth is new. It's a new chance to leave your mistakes, failures, and setbacks in the past. It's a new opportunity to do things better and different with your increased wisdom from the lessons you learned. It's a new moment to decide that you aren't going to be anxious about your schedule or your skills. Most importantly, it's a new chance to pause and ask God for His help.

I will lift up mine eyes unto the hills,
From whence cometh my help.
My help cometh from the LORD,
Which made heaven and earth.
Psalm 121:1-2 (KJV)

God made heaven and earth, so do you think He's incapable of taking your areas of limited knowledge (in comparison to His knowledge), and making them into something much greater?

Preparing for the Unknown

James 1:5 states, "If any of you lacks wisdom, you should ask God, who gives generously to all without finding fault, and it will be given to you." (NIV) God isn't judging you for not knowing, He's just waiting on you to ask.

Now I don't want to lose anybody who is reading this and has what they consider to be "just a job;" a place where they have no interest in outside of their paycheck - and there's nothing wrong with that. Sometimes we end up in positions that are just along the path to where we're truly called. I haven't forgotten about you and God most certainly has not - His wisdom for your unknown situation is still relevant.

This same all-knowing God knows when that movie producer is going to walk into your store, He knows when you'll get to meet that artist that you aspire to work alongside, He knows when that fashion designer will walk past you at your "uninteresting job" and take notice of you. That's why we are encouraged to be ready in season and out of season because our all-knowing God can show up with your next work blessing at any time and in any way.

Now I'm not saying don't do practical things to prepare for opportunities; I'm just saying *you need God to prepare* - if you want to prepare effectively. Why not seek him in advance on how to execute your work? Prepare daily and be prepared in every moment. As His children, we expect that at any time a good and gracious gift will come our way - especially if we have been spending the time with Him to ask Him and listen to what He's saying through His Word, visions He may give us, or a true word spoken by someone else.

Actions You Can Start Now

Begin your day with praise and worship. The Bible says, "Do not be anxious about anything, but in every situation, by prayer and petition, with thanksgiving, present your requests to God." Philippians 4:6 (NIV) Praise is a vital component in presenting your requests to God. If you are a parent, you may have grown accustomed to doing nice things for your children regularly (without receiving thanks or appreciation). How much greater and loved do you feel when you are approached with gratitude for all of the wonderful things you have done, sacrifices you have made, and resources you have provided? If praise brings us joy, don't you think that it brings God joy when we acknowledge Him and thank Him regularly? How often does He wake us up with the breath of life, provide food and other basic needs as well as our wants and desires... everyday, so we should at least thank Him everyday. Also, starting your day with praise, immediately shifts your perspective - it's hard to complain, or be worried about your schedule when you are focused on the good things God has done for you and singing out to Him. This isn't to diminish what you may be facing on that day and the stress or anxiety that you may be feeling about it. We've all been there. But as you begin to practice waking up with thanksgiving, you automatically position yourself for peace of mind.

Present your requests to God. As Ephesians 4:6 above states, by prayer and petition, present your requests to God. After you praise God, and you are in His presence with a heart of gratitude, pray and make your requests known. This is not about you giving God your to-do list and believing everything will be done as you want it. It's about presenting your plans, thoughts, and requests to God, acknowledging His complete control, and asking for His help to do what He wants you to do. God cares about what we care about, so there is nothing wrong with being completely honest with Him and bringing whatever you want to Him, as long as you approach Him with the love, respect, and honor He deserves as our Heavenly Father and Creator. And of course, these things will call for sacrifice on your behalf (you may have to get up earlier) but your mental well-being and Power in God throughout the day is worth it!

Chapter 2: Difficult Work Environments

> Look!" he said. "The people are united, and they all speak the same language. After this, nothing they set out to do will be impossible for them!" Genesis 11:6 (NLT)

"THE PEOPLE ARE UNITED."

People at work are diverse in their personalities, skills, values, and working styles. I have had the fortune of working with teams that have been highly collaborative and encouraging - and it's always great to find camaraderie amongst your work friends. But there's also another side of work environments that can be negative at times, which makes it extremely important to guard your interactions at work.

When I entered my first job out of college, I was bright-eyed and excited to embark on a new journey. All of us probably feel this same excitement at the prospect of a new opportunity. Usually in the early stages of a role there is more grace extended by co-workers and supervisors as you get up to speed, and people seem to be particularly nice. Then as you begin to settle into your role - more and more is unveiled to you.

Office politics... unveiled

Areas of disorganization... unveiled

Limitations for growth and promotion... unveiled

In the midst of unknown challenges that you may face at work, I can encourage you that there are some knowns that you can always be sure of:

1. *God will never leave you* nor forsake you (Deuteronomy 31:8)
2. *Greater is God* within you - His child - than anyone or anything that is within the world (1 John 4:4)
3. *God wants you to prosper*, and not just financially, but He wants your mind, will and emotional state to prosper (3 John 1:2)
4. The list could go on and on because, as His Word mentions, *God is SUPREME* over everything!

Difficult Work Environments

I have faced my share of difficult work environments and He was faithful to be with me through them all. At one workplace, the upper management yelled at, belittled, cursed, and second-guessed team members every day - all while keeping excessively long working hours. Now, I'm sure it may sound like I'm exaggerating or just complaining, but I can't even begin to describe the level of unprofessionalism that was displayed by the "leaders" of this team. Well, thankfully by the time I took the position, I was walking closely with God and being renewed regularly by studying His Word and going to small groups with other believers. This proved invaluable as I was able to hear about the victories that Christ was giving them in their personal and professional lives.

Thus, even though the team was being treated this horrible way, I was able to keep a cool head throughout the project. Now don't get me wrong, there were a few times that the stress did become overwhelming. But for the most part, I was able to keep my joy while working on that team. The joy of the Lord was definitely my strength during those times (Nehemiah 8:10).

On my last day of that project, the senior manager asked me how I was able to stay so calm during my time on the team. While I regret not giving God His proper glory at that time, the manager's question assured me that God's love and peace were illuminated in my life.

Regardless of how brutal work situations may have been at times, I had to learn that I couldn't use it as an excuse to sit around talking or complaining about it. I don't get to choose who I work with, but I can choose who I socialize with and how. I can choose to not be a part of the numerous opinions and side conversations that aren't always of the productive nature. That's my nice way of saying there can be much gossiping and grumbling within the workplace - I had to reach a point where I didn't allow myself to get pulled into those conversations, even with my "work friends." These conversations may seem innocent and harmless on the surface, but look at what the Word has to say:

Difficult Work Environments

> Do all things without grumbling and fault finding and complaining and questioning and doubting [among yourselves]. Philippians 2:14 (AMPCE)

> A gossip goes around telling secrets, but those who are trustworthy can keep a confidence. Proverbs 11:13 (NLT)

> Avoid godless chatter, because those who indulge in it will become more and more ungodly. 2 Timothy 2:16 (NIV)

I certainly don't want to become more and more ungodly. Well, that is what happens every time a person feeds into negative talk. And as tempting as it may have been to feed into negative discussions, I've had to learn to guard my conversations.

I won't pretend to be Miss Patty Perfect, there's been times when I didn't speak up - thinking that I wouldn't be affected if I just sat there. After all, I didn't want to cause conflict or be awkward about it, right? Proverbs 18:8 says, "The words of a gossip are like choice morsels;

they go down to the inmost parts." (NIV) Do I want the gossip of others to go down in my inmost parts? As much as I want to connect with people, there are times I have to remove myself from a conversation or change the subject to a positive note. The more I have done this, the more natural it becomes, and others are able to understand what type of conversations to involve me in.

> Remind the people to be subject to rulers and authorities, to be obedient, to be ready to do whatever is good, to slander no one, to be peaceable and considerate, and always to be gentle toward everyone.
>
> Titus 3:1-2 (NIV)

We cannot afford to give into something that's not beneficial to us or to others. Instead, it's important that we are lights in the workplace and pay attention to what we say.

> Do not let any unwholesome talk come out of your mouths, but only what is helpful for building others up according to their

needs, that it may benefit those who listen. Ephesians 4:29 (NIV)

If something or someone is truly bothering me, as uncomfortable as it may initially be, it is best to address it directly with the person in a professional manner. If that person has proven to be disrespectful in the past, then it may warrant escalating the issue to one of their superiors or HR. However, sitting around talking about it with other people is not going to make it better - it will make it worse, and leave the issues unresolved.

This needed to be addressed because sometimes we can make a difficult situation at work worse by feeding into the negativity. Be mindful about how you talk about situations and to whom - if you present your challenges to God, He will fight your battle, even if no one else does. You don't want to make God the last person you talk to about it. You also don't want to wait until the situation has gotten explosive to involve Him. He is still able to help, but why let things get that bad.

Work Freedom

Sometimes work environments may challenge our integrity - someone may request that you do something deceptive, or you may encounter a personal temptation. We must always choose to walk righteously. By righteously, I simply mean doing what is right. We know instinctively on the inside what is right and wrong - and if we are unsure, we can ask God to help us to make the decision. Romans 14:23 says that, "*If* you *do* anything you believe is not right, you are *sinning*," because you aren't following your convictions. (NLT) So, use the wisdom and help God gives you to walk in integrity towards your customers, co-workers, and company, but also practice integrity in who you are as a person. Clients and positions come and go, so if they try to take you off the path of who God has called you to be, then let them go because those interactions aren't beneficial for you anyways.

What happens when it's not your company or co-workers, but you that's making the work challenging. I have dealt with this debacle

Difficult Work Environments

throughout my career. If you are the type of person that is always motivated, running on 10 all day, and are unfamiliar with procrastination - then this may not resonate as much, but sometimes I just don't "feel like" working. Sometimes my why for the day is so distant that I can't muster up the energy, persuasion, or force to push past my feelings.

It can actually be quite an unpleasant situation - when you know that you need to get something done, you want to get it done, and you have everything to go ahead and do it - but you are unable to. Why wasn't I able to get it done? Personally, I've found that several things can be at play. 1. Analysis paralysis - I sit around thinking and dwelling so much on everything that needs to get done that I prolong doing it. 2. Perfectionism - I want it to be perfect to the extent that I end up nit-picking over things that aren't essential to focus on in the moment. 3. My work ethic. This one took me a while to recognize because I've always been ambitious and have gotten my work done, but if I look back, there has been a lack of intentionality in executing the work at times.

I learned over time that if I changed my work ethic, then completing tasks would seem less of a chore and more of an accomplishment. This didn't happen overnight and it's still an area of my life that I daily and continually place before God in surrender. You may think God only cares about the work we do in ministry, sharing the Gospel, or serving people on His behalf - but God also cares about the intricacies and details of our everyday work - no matter what that may be.

You pick up recycling bins? God cares about the details of how you do your work. You design clothes? God cares about the details. You cook food? God cares. You ring up customers at a register? God cares. You deliver training and development at an organization? God cares. The bible says, "Whatever you do [whatever your task may be], work from the soul [that is, put in your very best effort], as [something done] for the Lord and not for men." Colossians 3:23

Difficult Work Environments

(AMP). So as a representative of Christ, I knew I had to yield my internal struggles to Him, otherwise I wouldn't be able to fully walk in God's goodness on my job, and I would be misrepresenting Him with the work I do.

Actions You Can Start Now

Guard your thoughts and speech.

In surrendering your mind regarding work, you must guard your thoughts and speech. What does that mean? If it's not good or beneficial, don't think or say it. If it's not something that you would want someone thinking or saying about you, then it likely falls into the category of not being good and beneficial. If the thought is out of genuine care and concern about others' areas of improvement, then try saying a prayer in that moment - asking God to reveal this shortcoming to them and help them. You don't have to say a long prayer and you don't even have to say it out loud, but praying for them brings God into their situation and eliminates you sitting around thinking negative thoughts.

You can also meditate on scriptures when bad thoughts try to pop in your head during the workday: "When I first started, I would find myself needing to say this frequently (you'd be amazed at how many unpleasant thoughts a person may entertain throughout a day). I would just say to myself, "I cast down every imagination that exalts itself above the knowledge of God and I take captive every thought to make it obedient to Christ." (2 Corinthians 10:5) You can also try reminding yourself that you have the mind of Christ! (1 Corinthians 2:16) This also works if you get negative thoughts about yourself.

As you become more intentional about your thoughts and praying for others, it should help with how you speak about them as well.

Ask God for help daily

I've heard people say that they don't feel comfortable asking God for help with the "little things". They don't think they should be "bothering" Him about things that seem trivial in

Difficult Work Environments

their lives. Well, that couldn't be the furthest thing from the truth.

The bible says, where does my help come from - all of my help comes from the Lord. This means that *all your help* comes from the Lord. In times when you are challenged in completing your work and don't think you have the strength or knowledge to do it - pause and say God help me "x,y,z". You may not feel like anything has changed immediately, but if you press through and allow God to show up, He will. He will honor that in your moment of need, you thought to call on Him.

Practice asking God for help in everything you do; you will be in awe to see just how willing God is to help you out, no matter how big or small the task may seem.

Chapter 3: Fighting Off Discontentment

I reached a point in my job, as many people may, where I became discontent. Was I discontent with the work; had it suddenly become dull or boring? Or was I discontent with me and how I was functioning from day-to-day? These were real questions that I had to face, and find a way to push past, because I knew that they would take a toll on my job if I didn't. I couldn't afford that because after all, my job seemed to be my livelihood.

It would be nice to sit here and tell you that I sat down, reflected on the situation, and took a good look in the mirror to identify what was wrong and move forward - but that's not the case. What I will say is that I did begin to pray and ask God about these feelings that I was experiencing. I wanted to know - was this a sign -

a sign of this not being the right job for me anymore. "Lord if I'm this unhappy, is it because it's time for me to leave this job and do something else?" It was a real question that I had.

For those of you who absolutely love their jobs - I will provide some additional insight into what I mean when I say discontent. I was dissatisfied with corporate and team dynamics, and the ever-present striving to be noticed, recognized, and rewarded for contributions to the team. I was dissatisfied with being on someone else's time and blatant disrespect of mine at times - getting there at the top of the morning and leaving in the wee hours of the night. I was dissatisfied with the constant discomfort - the discomfort of knowing that I didn't talk like my teammates, I didn't look like my teammates, and in ways couldn't relate to them and vice versa.

This weighed heavily on me because work is where I spent most of my day and time. Work likely consumes the majority of the week for

Fighting Off Discontentment

most people. Thanks to technology, I oftentimes carried it home with me or to my hotel (since I traveled a lot for work). Work was constantly with me and so were the individuals who could access me through email or text and attempt to reach me at any point in time. It seemed to be a nagging thorn in my flesh that I just could not escape.

How could I reconcile these feelings given that I prayed for the opportunity? The Lord was gracious enough to give me the amazing job that compensated well and was somewhat interesting (by most people's standards). How could I even begin to complain? I couldn't complain and I certainly felt that there was no place to be discontent. I recognized the blessing of the job and ultimately knew that the discontentment was internal.

The discontentment didn't have anything to do with the role that I was in, the people that I was around, or even the time that was being used. It was all internal - internal insecurities that were staring me in the face day-to-day: why am I here, how did I end up here, and do I have what it takes to excel in this role. I optimistically wanted to believe that I could do it - and *I knew I could do it*. After all, I can do all things through Christ Who strengthens me. I was only able to make it as far as I did because of Him, but I made a mistake.

At some point I turned my eyes away from He to me. At some point in my career, on this job, and in these roles I begin to think about myself - what I was able to do, what I was able to accomplish, and who I was able to please. Me. Me. Me. I'm sure that happens often - we are aware of our need for God in the beginning only to lose sight of Him along the way. I would pray and call out to God for these wonderful opportunities and awards, get them, and then lean to my own strength.

I extend myself grace of course because I didn't know then. I didn't know that I wasn't supposed to ask God for the blessing and then just try to take care of it myself once I got it. Made sense to me at the time - why would I ask

Fighting Off Discontentment

God for something that I didn't think I could handle on my own? That's at least what my worldly reasoning told me. But Thank God that His thoughts are not our thoughts, and His ways are not our ways. In this journey to seeking Work Freedom, God unveiled to me that it truly is the opposite. He is the Beginning and the End, and He desires to be involved from the Beginning to the End.

It is not a burden to lean on God. His Word tells us over and over to lean on Him, that He cares, and to cast our burdens unto Him. This is hard for a lot of people to do - of course I'm not saying that I would ever try to intentionally hold onto a hardship - but relinquishing control doesn't just happen automatically.

So, there I was with my discontentment and my shame for feeling like I wasn't able to give my all and be the best, enthusiastic person that I could be for the role. What's a girl to do? I did what most of us who are facing a tough situation would try to do - press through it. I kept going to work, getting done what I could, being a light to those around me and helping where I felt capable. Which was good; it was good for me to do those things, but I was still missing something in so many ways because I was not resolving the issue.

God had to show me throughout the course of my career that the only way to overcome discontentment is through Him. I was discontent because I was trying to orchestrate a life that I never created, and I was too busy looking at my own limitations. Once I realized how truly limitless I was - to do and be everything that God planned for me - I became excited to take the steps I needed to move forward.

<u>Prayer</u>

Lord, I thank You that *You want the very best* for me and that *I have the very best*. While I wait patiently for everything to come to pass, I ask You to fill me with Your joy. Awaken me every morning with your joy so that no matter what I face in my day, I have a contentment that is unshakeable and unmoved by my experiences. Where I have areas of discontentment in my life, Father give me the

Fighting Off Discontentment

wisdom to know what I need to change, what I need to remove myself from, what I need to challenge myself to do, and when I should be still. I'm grateful for Your love and excited about my present and my future - as you unveil your plans to me. In the Name of Jesus I pray, Amen!

Chapter 4: Getting Past Worry & Doubt

Some may wonder why I didn't just leave and explore other options if I wasn't happy at my job. That is where worry and doubt come in. Although I knew something was off and I knew that a change needed to be made, I wasn't willing to take the steps forward past my current situation because of worry and doubt.

I was worried about getting someone to hire me, thus being able to maintain my "steady" income. I also couldn't think of an alternative job that I would be content in or felt confident enough to get "easily".

I'll be honest, I struggled with a lot of self-doubt back then. I was fearful coming into most employment and corporate opportunities, which is still something I monitor today - making sure that those thoughts don't creep back in. For instance, with every interview I faced, I was deathly afraid. I was reserved in real life and definitely not accustomed to talking about myself and my accomplishments. I considered it to be boastful and felt extremely uncomfortable going into a session to "sell myself" and talk about how wonderful and great of an employee I would be.

How was I going to do that if I was unsure of how wonderful and great of an employee I actually was? I knew I was capable and could get the work done but I was ever aware of my areas of improvement and insecurities. So much so, that I begin to lose sight of my traits that did make me stand out and greatly contribute to organizations.

Luckily, I did not have to make the decision to leave because I was laid off my job. I can say luckily now because I know how God used that entire process to purge certain ways and thoughts out of me that were not for His glory or my benefit. The transition also helped me to step out in ways that I never would have if I stayed holding onto the safety blanket of false job security.

Initially, I was excited to have a fresh start, but quickly that excitement for new possibilities turned into a crippling and debilitating stagnation. I became so consumed with my insufficiencies that I didn't feel worthy to do anything - I kept thinking how and why a new role wouldn't work out. Which, in my head, was confirmed when I would receive rejections from companies that I applied to. Every time I interviewed with them, they would ask why I left my last company, and I would replay the guilt and shame of the failed opportunity over-and-over again. Now that I'm more mature in my career, I understand that lay-offs happen, and many times at no fault of that particular person. I also know that many people experience it - even the most successful. However, being my first job out of college, it truly proved to be a devastating blow.

Work Freedom

At that particular time, I was a part of a young professionals group in Atlanta called The Winner's Circle. The Lord had given me guidance to start consulting on my own, first in my field, Change Management, and then working with startups. I would tell everyone in the group about my plans and what I was going to do with my business and everyone was cheering me on and very supportive. The problem was that I was scared beyond belief - how was I going to go and do something that I failed at in another company? How was I going to help others start a company when it was my first time starting myself? I made tiny steps here and there, but as time went on I became discouraged.

There's this thing called imposter syndrome, "also called perceived fraudulence, [which] involves feelings of self-doubt and personal incompetence that persist despite your education, experience, and accomplishments."

Imposter Syndrome. (2021, April 16). In *Healthline Mental Health*. Retrieved from https://www.healthline.com/health/mental-health/imposter-syndrome#takeaway

Getting Past Worry and Doubt

Basically, I did not feel qualified at all to do what God was calling me to and I honestly felt like a fake saying that I was going to do it. I eventually pulled away from The Winner's Circle organization and my position heading the Professional Development Committee because I felt like anything but a winner.

Self-doubt can cause a person to spend day-after-day lost in negative thoughts about what they want to do and immediately shutting down progress by reflecting on why they can't do it. That's what happened to me; I became so lost in my negative fear, doubt, and shame that days went by, weeks went by, months went by, years (yes years) went by with little to no forward movement in my professional career.

I will say that my saving grace during this time was that I continued to serve in my church, which was a blessing because it didn't completely isolate me and still allowed me to have some sense of purpose and encouragement - however small it may have seemed at the time. Not working - is a drain on life - and something I had never envisioned for myself as a young, single, ambitious woman. Here I was at home, laid out on a sofa, watching TV all day, or playing video games, which worried me even more. I remember being in my home alone, on my living room floor one night just feeling completely broken and sobbing so hard that I couldn't catch my breath - I was crying so hard that I couldn't breathe and I wondered - is this it? Did I reach my prime? Is God going to take my life away since I'm not making any good use of it? But I wasn't alone - God was with me in that moment - my very present help and comfort - letting me know that I shall live and not die. In whatever struggles you may face, no matter how big or small - you shall live because the Greater One lives in You, and unlike a job, that cannot be taken away.

Being in that state took its toll both financially and emotionally. Gifts are my love language, and I prided myself on being generous. After all the bible does say, "the godly are generous givers." Psalms 37:21 (NLT) I had a desire to give

- not just of my time - but I also wanted to be a financial blessing as well. It's one thing to choose whether or not you will give into the work of the Kingdom of God through church or an organization, but it's a whole other feeling to want to give, but not have it to give.

    I was saying to myself, "Lord, I used to tithe every paycheck, so why am I in this position to where I don't have a job and the means to give?" Well God did indeed answer that for me. I had taken my eyes off Who had given me the seed (the money) to share in the first place - and placed my focus on my job. I was desperate to get back to having a "steady" stream of income so I could take care of my needs and wants, including giving into the Body of Christ. It wasn't until I had the revelation that the income came from God all along, and began to seek Him for direct provision, that I was able to receive with the right heart and mind. I sought Him by acknowledging Him in the situation, praying to Him continually, asking for His help, and reading the Bible to hear His guidance.

Work Freedom

I wanted to tithe and feel like I was "contributing" to the point that I began to tithe using credit. In hindsight, I find that to be contrary to what God has told me about being a lender, not a borrower. The Word even goes as far to say that the borrower is slave to the lender - as believers in Christ we are called to be free, not a slave to anything except for righteousness. The bible says, "Owe no man any thing, but to love one another: for he that loveth another hath fulfilled the law." Romans 13:8 (KJV)

Once I got that revelation I stopped giving on credit and began trusting God to provide - and God did indeed restore. As I eventually started back working, He allowed me to pay off the over $20,000 in credit card debt that I accrued during the years that I didn't have a job. I would be remiss if I didn't mention that my village around me not only encouraged me in my low places, but also blessed me financially as well, especially one of my greatest supporters, my dad.

Getting Past Worry and Doubt

I remember one Sunday at church someone randomly gave me five dollars - now five dollars may seem so trivial, but it was such a blessing in that moment. I'm sure that person didn't even realize it. I went and got food for that week (I'm a vegetarian, so I can get a bundle of kale, carrots, onions, peppers, pasta, all for a dollar or less each and eat pretty good). You never know. What seems like a small word of encouragement or financial blessing - could be something so special for someone going through a wilderness season.

Also, and this is a side note, this gesture showed me that you can't judge what you think someone has or can do based on external appearances. I was pulling up to church every Sunday in a Mercedes (that I couldn't pay for out of my pocket at the time); what if that person decided not to give, thinking they knew my financial circumstance? That's why it's important to be faithful and obedient in what God tells us. God gives us the honor to refresh each other and help each other in need.

True story: I purchased that car in August and lost my job in October in that same year. I don't say that because woe is me. I praise God because this was just one of the many ways that God demonstrated that He would keep and sustain me no matter what. I was never lacking in anyway, and I was able to pay that same car off last year (a year after being able to pay off all of my credit debt). God is faithful, so when we face the temptation to doubt and worry, we can truly trust Him to come through.

<u>Actions You Can Start Now</u>

Declare What You Know

If you have moments that you begin to doubt and say, "I don't know how this will turn out", or "I don't know if I can do this," or in any way feel uncertain about your future, you can focus in on what you do know. When I would begin to say what I don't know, the Lord would immediately tell me to say "I do know"… and so do you. The book of Romans reminds us, "we know that in all things God works for the good of those who love him, who have been called according to his purpose" Romans 8:28 (NIV). So if you love Christ and have made the decision to surrender your life to Him, you are called according to His purpose and know that He is working *all things for good* on your behalf.

Dismiss Lies and Negative Self-talk

Extend grace to yourself if you begin to experience fear or doubt. Know that you are probably being hard on yourself or overthinking the situation. If there are truly changes that need to be made then allow yourself to acknowledge it, reflect on all that you have accomplished and the skills that it took to get there, then make a plan to move forward.

You are contributing.
Your very existence here is contributing.
You are still usable and valuable.

Chapter 5: Seeking Purpose & Passion

Purpose is what God wants me to do; or better yet, what He created me with the intention to do. Ephesians 2:10 says, "for we are God's handiwork, created in Christ Jesus to do good works, which God prepared in advance for us to do." (NIV) So, God already prepared work for me to do before I even got here. This truth placed the desire in me to figure out what that work was.

Growing up, I may have occasionally heard the word purpose - maybe. More often, people asked me what I wanted to be when I grew up - which would lead me to fantasize about a life that I viewed enjoyable like cooking or singing. As I got older and could understand a little more about the realities of livelihood, my ideal vision of work morphed into jobs that I viewed as being stable. The jobs that would allow me to securely have the essentials like good shelter, food, clothes, etc. However, this focus on "what I wanted to be" and "how I planned to create stability" completely left God out of the picture.

Sure I had a relationship with God and I prayed to Him regarding everything - but this narrow focus left my prayers along the lines of "Lord give me what I want" instead of "Lord show me what I was created for." I think all of us eventually hit a place where we begin to understand what purpose is and our need to personally find it. Otherwise, we find ourselves doing what we set out to do, but never truly finding fulfillment in it because it isn't our ultimate assignment.

The great thing is that God truly does work all things together for good (Romans 8:28). As I look over my life, I am able to see how every opportunity, educational experience, and job from my past, has positioned me to be successful at what God placed me here to do. The other wonderful thing is that once I came to the realization that I needed to seek God for my specific purpose, He was faithful to begin revealing those things to me. Matthew 7:7 says, "Ask and it will be given to you; seek and you will find; knock and the door will be opened to you." (NIV) God continues to reveal His purpose for my life - year by year - as I take steps in faith towards what He is leading me to do.

Passion is what I like to do; the things I feel strongly about. Throughout my life, I always found it hard to pinpoint what I was "passionate" about. I knew I loved food - both cooking and eating - and I've always had a heart to serve and help those in need, but when asked to examine what I was passionate about from a work context, I found it hard to identify. I guess that's why they say if you do what you love, you never work a day in your life.

Well in my case, I viewed a job as a job - not something I was necessarily passionate about, but a necessity to get the things that I needed and wanted in life. So how did I begin to understand what I was passionate about? For me, it went back to seeking God about my purpose. God will give us a passion for the things that we are purposed to do. Philippians 2:13 says, "For God is working in you, giving you the desire and the power to do what pleases him." (NLT) Thus, the more I sought after and began to understand my purpose, the more I became excited (and passionate) about my assignments and the impacts it would have on my life and the lives of others.

<u>Actions You Can Start Now</u>

Get an Accountability Partner

Connect with someone who will help push you towards understanding and walking in your God-given purpose. Someone you can also encourage in their walk. I have a friend that I talk with at the beginning and end of each week. She's asked me to give her feedback about her strengths and ideas, and she's given me practical tips on prioritizing. As humans, we need suitable helpers, so identify someone who can be a suitable helper in your life and create a routine that works for the two of you.

Just Ask

If you are uncertain about what your purpose is, then ask God. If you are not sure of what you are passionate about, then ask God. If you know your purpose but feel overwhelmed with the idea of carrying it out, then ask God for the resources and steps to walk it out. I don't want to oversimplify things, because your purpose is such an important aspect of life - but in this case it is as simple as persistently asking God to reveal these things and help you along the way. The key is to believe that He will show you and that He will help you.

"If any of you lacks wisdom, you should ask God, who gives generously to all without finding fault, and it will be given to you. But when you ask, you must believe and not doubt, because the one who doubts is like a wave of the sea, blown and tossed by the wind. That person should not expect to receive anything from the Lord. Such a person is double-minded and unstable in all they do." James 1:5-8 (NIV)

So let yourself be of one-mind, focused on God, allowing Him to reveal the purpose He created you for and ignite the passion for it inside of you! Then pay attention to the opportunities and connections that God begins to place around you - what areas is He wanting you to grow and expand yourself in? What areas is He revealing are past its season in your life?

Chapter 6: Managing Frustration

We would love if things always went our way; exactly how we planned, envisioned, or wanted it to be. However, that is not the reality of life - and work is no exception. We will face disappointments, annoyances, and what seem like roadblocks, but we don't have to stay in that place of frustration. We have the power to look at the situation from a different perspective and bring our frustrations before God. His Word says, "Do not be anxious about anything, but in every situation, by prayer and petition, with thanksgiving, present your requests to God. And the peace of God, which transcends all understanding, will guard your hearts and your minds in Christ Jesus." Philippians 4:6-7 (NIV)

Frustration can come in many forms, but one of the biggest areas of frustration for me has been regarding timing. For instance, in my first job out of school, I became frustrated with my progression in the role. In certain positions, especially in business settings, there is an expectation that the longer you are with the company, the greater responsibility you take on - and the greater your pay and title. Project after project I would get good feedback from my supervisors, but when it came to the overall project - my work contributions were not deemed significant enough.

Could I have done more to ensure leaders were aware of and valued my work? Absolutely. I could have made sure that I secured advocates that would go to bat for me in the promotion calls - but honestly, I didn't want to. At the time, I didn't want to be "strategic" about my work relationships. I wanted to do good work and let that speak for itself. Unfortunately, that's not the world that we live in. Key decisions in all areas of life are forged based on relationships.

Now I say "unfortunately," but now that I've grown in life and my career, my mind has shifted to know that fortunately our outcomes are determined by our relationships. Most notably - our relationship with God. The same way that my co-workers used their connections to their advantage, is the same way that we as believers in Christ, can use our relationship with Him to our advantage.

God is referenced throughout the bible as being Supreme, Sovereign, The King of all kings and The Lord of all lords, so we are connected to the Highest of all decision-makers. Does this mean that we will get everything that we go after? No, but it does mean that Our God will not withhold good from us, so as we partner with Him, He will give us favor with others and elevate us above what any person can do.

Relationships with others are also important - not for what they can do for us - but because God is relational. The whole reason He sent Christ is to be reconciled with us, so we should at least seek to be a light just as Jesus was. When we work with others we need to see them as people - with their own unique experiences, desires, and frustrations - have empathy for them, and know that it is a blessing to help out one another.

I've also been frustrated wondering when new opportunities and doors would open for me. I went through a prolonged time, when I began to look for work and no matter what position I was applying to (positions I knew I was more than qualified for), I wasn't hearing anything back from anyone. No emails, phone calls, interview requests - nothing. What was wrong? 1) There is a time for everything. There was still time that I needed to grow in trusting God instead of a job and mentally prepare to enter a new season of work. 2) There was a plan and steps that I needed to surrender to God and take action by faith in order to get to the next level that I wanted to go.

In that moment, I felt the frustration of not being able to provide, but all the more I understood that a self-sufficient mentality about finances got me into the issue in the first place. That moment of frustration - was just that - a moment. Something that would be minor in comparison to the accomplishments and victories that God had already allowed me to have and the wins that were to come.

We don't always get what we ask, when we ask it, but God gives us what is best and needed in that moment. That is why everything points back to keeping our eyes focused on Jesus and understanding what the Lord has already done and wants to do in this upcoming time in our lives.

For some, they may already be faithfully walking in what God told them to do and they are experiencing frustration about when things will "take off." There's much to be said about perseverance and you can't persevere in something that you have only been doing momentarily. James 1:4 says, "Let perseverance finish its work so that you may be mature and complete, not lacking anything." (NIV) I'm a personal witness that I needed to grow in maturity in my work habits - prioritizing tasks, overcoming procrastination, and taking greater ownership - just to name a few. Those things needed to mature in me so that I wouldn't be lacking when things "take off" and "go to the next level." The King James Version puts it this way, "But let patience have her perfect work, that ye may be perfect and entire, wanting nothing." You can't be frustrated and "wanting nothing" at the same time, so choose one and ask God to help you build patience. As opportunities begin to come, rely on God's strength and the promise of a good outcome to help you press forward.

<u>Actions You Can Start Now</u>
Get away for a moment

Sometimes taking a vacation, sabbatical, or even a couple of days off, can give you time to get a better perspective on your situation. You can begin to decipher whether your frustrations are based on internal unmet expectations or if the frustrations are issues that need to be addressed with others involved. Stepping away from the situation can help you know if this is something I should appreciate more or an indication that a change needs to be made.

Managing Frustration

Taking a moment to yourself can also include activities that allow you to reset your mind and let go of the frustrations. You personally know what brings you solace - it could be a long soak in the tub, a kick boxing session, or a walk around the neighborhood.

Talk it out with trusted advisors

Identify others who have familiarity with your line of work or the wisdom to give you objective advice that you may not have thought of yourself. There are times when we could just be over or under-thinking something that we are doing. Proverbs 15:22 says, "Without consultation and wise advice, plans are frustrated, But with many counselors they are established and succeed." (AMP) Of course our #1 advisor should always be the Holy Spirit, so bring all advice given to you and all frustrations about the situation to Him, and trust what He is internally leading you to do. God will often confirm what He's saying three times - it could be through His Word, a word from others, or something that you are watching or listening to.

Work Freedom

Do not limit the ways that God can speak to you or underestimate the comfort that He can provide during those times of frustration.

Chapter 7: Focusing on What's Important

So what's important? We all have a God-given purpose, as previously discussed, so carrying out the mission that God sends us here to accomplish is of the upmost importance. I reached a point in my life where I was desperate to know the assignments God had for me to complete. Once I got past the "doing it with fear and trembling" stage (also known as "trying to do it in my own strength") and began to seek Him first, I was able to take everything the Lord was giving me and prioritize.

Proverbs 3:6 says to "Seek his will in all you do, and he will show you which path to take." (NLT) Jesus likewise stated that we should seek first the Kingdom of God and all things we need in this life will be added to us (Matthew 5:33). So, if we prioritize going to God first - asking Him what to do and the steps we need to take - He will direct our path in that area. Jesus said, "I have brought you glory by completing the work you gave me to do." John 17:4 (NIV) We must also make it a priority to complete the work that God gives us to do.

As good as my intentions have been over the years, a lot of the assignments that God has given me were put on the back burner. Not because I don't have reverence for Him or want Him to use me in this world for good, but honestly it was a matter of mismanaged time.

I just never seemed to have enough time to do it. I spent a good amount of time doing (or thinking about) my "9 to 5" work - which sometimes ended up being "8 am - 11 pm" work, depending on the project. I noticed that I spent significant time eating and snacking. I also needed some time to "unwind" by watching hours of tv, movies, and YouTube, or dancing around the room, or scrolling through social media - you know, the important stuff. Then I was tired. When on earth would I possibly be able to

Focusing On What's Important

do these "other things" that God wanted me to do?

It wasn't until I started to give God the first of my day that I was eventually able to see the importance of giving Him the first of my work. What do I mean by this? Everyone who has a job or career has a purpose there (even if it is a temporary season). I began to seek God about how He wanted me to use my career and positions to bring Him glory. I did the same with the other assignments, goals, and business ideas that God had given me.

I asked God to show me how they all come together, which ones I should focus on, and how I should go about getting them done. In doing so, God began to show me the urgency of some things over others and the ease of setting up particular items. Essentially, God allowed me to prioritize the activities that would lay the foundation for each area He called me to, so I could then prioritize building out those respective areas.

Work Freedom

If you ask God for divine strategy for work, He will give you the vision and provide you with the steps (if you keep seeking and asking along the way). Since the foundation that you are laying is God, every aspect of what you are building will be shown for what it is. What I have come to realize is that divine strategies yield divine results. 1 Corinthians 3:13 says that "fire will reveal what kind of work each builder has done. The fire will show if a person's work has any value." (NLT) When your work is put to the fire and the quality of it is tested, the value of what has been done will be evident. So if God is the foundation, you will be able to see the value that you brought in the end - even if the outcome wasn't what you desired or expected.

Not every work opportunity, project, or business endeavor has the "perfect ending." That doesn't mean it did not play an important part in your learning, growing, contributing, and being able to move to the next level that He's taking you. I put God first now, even when I'm "in a hurry" or think I might miss out on something.

Focusing On What's Important

Anytime with God is good time and the more time you spend with Him and see how He's moving in Your life, the more you begin to do whatever you need to clear that time. Time, by the way, that already belongs to Him because He gave you every second of every day.

I also know sometimes we can second-guess whether we are truly hearing from God or making the right moves, but God is faithful to redirect us if we are misled. Psalms 119:133 says, "Guide my steps by your word, so I will not be overcome by evil." (NLT) When you make it a point to read His Word, He will illuminate things that you may not otherwise see. This can give you the insight that will help you with your work that day or He may confirm something that you already believed He was leading you to.

Some people may think the bible is outdated or cannot apply to their situation, but they would be surprised. There have been countless times I asked God about something I was unclear of or worried about and began to read His Word -

and that very passage that I "happened" to read spoke to me about my very situation.

God is very creative when it comes to speaking to us. Even Jesus spoke in parables to the people, so yes God can use the same scripture that you have previously read numerous times to speak to you in new ways. The Word of God is described as being, "Alive and active. Sharper than any double-edged sword…it judges the thoughts and attitudes of the heart." Hebrews 4:12 (NIV) Putting God first means making it a priority to spend time in His Word. Christ is the Living Word, so time in His Word is time spent with Him.

Once I had settled that God had to be first in my work - not just in thought, but also action - God began to show me the importance of my continued learning and development. I do not know if anyone else is like I was, but I will shamelessly say that the only training or learning I used to do for work was training that was mandatory. I was under the impression that once

Focusing On What's Important

I graduated school, I had checked the education box, and now I had moved on to the work box.

I was typically just "going through the motions" when it came to education. I had a huge awakening once I realized how much intentional learning I needed in order to progress in my work. God showed me that in order to grow and gain confidence in my field, I would have to be intentional about learning.

For those who already live a scholarly life, don't check out on me yet - we can only get so far with our studies. Yes, we can take our skillset to a certain level through conventional lessons and literature, but God can take us so much farther.

God gives us the special skills that we need to advance in our craft. After God instructed the Israelites to build the Ark of the Covenant and all its furnishings, the Lord assured Moses that the work was in capable hands saying, "I have filled him with the Holy Spirit of God, giving him great wisdom, ability, and expertise in all kinds of crafts... I have given special skill to all the gifted craftsmen so they can make all things I have commanded you to make." Exodus 31:3,6b (NLT) So God does not just tell us to do something, but He also gives us the means to do it. We need the Spirit of God to get the work done and we have the Spirit of God - for those who accept Christ as Lord over their lives and Savior of this world. We have the skills needed to get the work done.

In building our skillset, God also uses the people that He places in our lives to model what we need to grow in. In Philippians, Paul encourages the believers in Christ to, "keep putting into practice all you learned and received from me - everything you heard from me and saw me doing. Then the God of peace will be with you." Philippians 4:9 (NLT) When I was first laid off and asked God what I should do next, He told me to consult independently in my field; He later told me to start consulting with startup owners. Both times I took steps - full of doubt that I would be able to do it. Years later, after my faith and confidence in Him had been built up, He allowed me to work under someone in my field that I could glean from. Eventually, I also met someone who had experience consulting startups and small businesses - and what do you know, they happened to be looking for an apprentice. Both were seasoned professionals who helped me to see that I could walk in everything God was calling me to; I just couldn't be afraid to put myself out there. This is a side note, but I want you to know that this did not happen overnight; both these occurrences took time. Know that God is always working in the background and foreground, setting people and opportunities in place at the right time.

God not only gives us special skills and helps us to learn new ones, but He is faithful to use the skills we already have. One of Jesus' twelve disciples, Peter, was a fisherman by trade. One day when the need arose for them to pay taxes, Jesus told Peter to, "Go to the lake and throw out your line. Take the first fish you catch; open its mouth and you will find a four-drachma coin. Take it to them for my tax and yours." So Jesus had Peter use his skills as a fisherman to go out to a lake and catch a fish for them to pay their taxes. God moved in a supernatural way - He provided the money, not by Peter selling the fish he caught, but in an unconventional way. God will bless our skills in unconventional ways. Not to mention, God supplied all they needed for the taxes in the first catch!

That was not the first or only time we see Jesus put Peter to work in a miraculous way. Luke 5 tells the account of when Jesus calls Peter as a disciple. Jesus was preaching to a crowd and asked to sit in Peter's boat while He did so. After He finished preaching, He told Peter to,

> "'Put out into deep water and let down the nets for a catch.' Simon answered, 'Master, we've worked hard all night and haven't caught anything. But because you say so, I will let down the nets.' When they had done so, they caught such a large number of fish that their nets began to break." Luke 5:4-6 (NIV)

Focusing On What's Important

Do not underestimate how God can take what He has already given - the capabilities, tools, and position - to bless you with so much more. There are things that I am doing now, getting paid exceedingly more than when I was trying to do things in my own strength and in a different timing.

Lastly, I could not discuss focusing on what's important without addressing the big elephant in the room - money, money, money. I would be inauthentic if I didn't discuss where compensation falls into all of this. Especially, since money is usually the driver behind a lot of work decisions: what roles we take, what ventures we go into, who we hire. I recognize that money is to be valued, but not valued over obedience to what God is telling you to do.

I think people - including myself at times - can get tripped up thinking that a God path is not necessarily a lucrative and successful one. But why would He do that? Success can come in many forms outside of money - but the God of splendor and majesty that I read about in the

Word - gives abundantly (John 10:10), has good gifts for His children (Matthew 7:11), withholds no good thing (Psalms 84:11) and would not send you on a path that will leave you in lack, unable to take care of your needs, and unable to help others.

I already discussed my season with little to no income - however, during that time I never lacked anything that I needed. What money I didn't have to give, I was still able to give in time by serving in the House of God to advance His Kingdom. Plus, that season only served to make me more financially savvy and a better steward of my money in the seasons to follow. Jesus came down to earth and made Himself poor so that we may be rich (2 Corinthians 8:9). Rich means rich in every sense of my life, including my finances. We have to *choose to* walk in Him and not think that our own ways or understanding are better than His.

Maybe it's not money for you - maybe you treasure recognition or elevation. I realized that the significance in my work did not come from rising up the ranks, but being where I'm supposed to be, doing what I'm supposed to do. I don't need to have the fancy title. While Jesus was here on this earth, the people kept trying to seize Him and make Him into an earthly king, but Jesus told the people that He came here to serve. So let God promote you to the places that He wants you to go and don't let others pressure you to fulfill their plan for your life - if it does not align to God's. You can't be willing to do everything that others want you to do, even if it's something "good."

Always examine your why. It should always align to God's will and trace back to Him as the driving force.

<u>Actions You Can Start Now</u>
Create Alone-Time with God

Jesus often went up on a mountain alone to pray - and you also need designated space where you can retreat to God and focus in on what He is saying.

Chapter 8: Faith + Works is Alive

We are the seeds of Abraham. Galatians 3:29 states that, "If you belong to Christ, then you are Abraham's seed, and heirs according to the promise." (NIV) In Genesis we learn that seeds sown produce the same kind: Seeds of love towards others produces love shown towards you. Seeds of finances sown into the Kingdom of God produces increased financial provision. Seeds of faith in God produces the substance of what we are hoping for. So as seeds of Abraham, we produce the same kind of faith.

Scripture goes into great detail regarding the faith that Abraham had - and the Bible is filled with many others like him - but let's look at some examples of his faith:

"It was by faith that Abraham obeyed when God called him to leave home and go to another land that God would give him as his inheritance. He went without knowing where he was going. And even when he reached the land God promised him, he lived there by faith—for he was like a foreigner, living in tents. And so did Isaac and Jacob, who inherited the same promise."
Hebrews 11:8-9 (NLT)

Abraham's faith caused him to go somewhere God told him to go with no information and stay somewhere God told him to stay, even though the conditions were not the best.

"It was by faith that Abraham offered Isaac as a sacrifice when God was testing him. Abraham, who had received God's promises, was ready to sacrifice his only son, Isaac, even though God had told him, 'Isaac is the son through whom your descendants will be counted.' Abraham reasoned that if Isaac died, God was able to bring him back to life again. And in a sense, Abraham did receive his son back from the dead."

Hebrews 11:17-19 (NLT)

Abraham was willing to sacrifice his family and loved one for God because he believed that God would come through and make it better in the end. His faith brought, what looked to be a dead outcome, back to life.

Let's look at another person associated with Abraham - rarely praised for her faith, but relatable in many ways. In Genesis 16, we see Hagar who has found herself in a dire situation after leaving her place of work. Hagar was an Egyptian servant who worked for Abram and Sarai - and under their direction became a wife to Abram in order to bear him a son. However, Hagar began to feel contempt towards Sarai once she became pregnant.

Perhaps we can relate to Hagar - being in a position, doing what we are asked, but then beginning to feel contempt because the role became something that we didn't ask for. Or maybe you have been on another side like I

Work Freedom

have - being prideful and feeling like what I'm carrying is more important than what my current role reflects. In either case, Hagar found herself in a less than desirable position and her contempt about it led to harsh treatment from Sarai. Sarai treated her harshly until she finally ran away. That happens today as well - some people will treat you harshly at work, hoping you will run away too.

So let's recap where Hagar is so far, because she faces quite a bit. Her employers told her to do something. She did it, then felt contempt about the situation. She was treated harshly. She ran away. Then God reassured her that He saw her and that He heard her - which would become the name of her son, Ishmael (meaning God hears). So Hagar follows the instruction of the Lord, returns, and submits to authority.

Five chapters later in Genesis 21, we again see Hagar - this time she's been fired and kicked to the curb with her son. She's wandering aimlessly in the desert and has run out of resources. Thinking her situation was at the brink of death - she gave up. It was in that moment that an angel of God spoke to her - he told her that God heard the boy crying, asked her what was wrong, told her not to be afraid, then assured her that He would still make her son into a great nation and gave them water so they would not die.

That is the level of care and comfort the Lord gives us - even when it seems we are at our breaking point. In fact, although Ishmael is usually known for being Abraham's illegitimate son, before Hagar and Ishmael left that day, God told Abraham that, "I will also make a nation of the descendants of Hagar's son because he is your son, too." Genesis 21:13 (NLT) So even when other people try to disqualify us, and cancel out what is rightfully our inheritance, God shows up and lets us know that He will still do something great in our lives because of Who Our Father is.

I wanted to share those examples of faith to show you the faith that these individuals had in what God was saying to them, how they responded, and the outcomes. Like them, we must also put action to our faith to see our work come alive.

When you have faith in something, you can see what you believe will happen. James 2:18 says, "But someone may say, 'You [claim to] have faith and I have [good] works; show me your [alleged] faith without the works [if you can], and I will show you my faith by my works [that is, by what I do]." (AMP) So when I say you can see what you believe - I don't mean with your natural eye. When you have faith, your belief is already so much of a reality to you that you can envision it. Beyond envisioning it, you also move and operate as if it is surely yours - because it is, by faith.

Now does this mean that you get everything you want, how you want it, when you want it? No. That could be for many reasons, including your motives - but let's assume we are talking about something that you know to be in line with His promises to you. The answer is still no because God loves us too much to leave us in

Faith + Works is Alive

this world without the essential tools we need to be successful in life. One such tool is discussed in James 1:3, which says, "For you know that when your faith is tested, your endurance has a chance to grow." So as we practice our faith for the vision God has given us, we build endurance. We will need this endurance because it allows us to stand strong with God in the midst of obstacles, challenges, and roadblocks that we are likely to face on this road called life.

How do you know what actions to take to accompany your faith? The bible says much about where we get the steps and how we take them. The Lord gave me a very vivid illustration of this on Thanksgiving. I was walking down the stairs at my house, listening to music, and preparing to get my food going. As I was nearing the bottom, I apparently missed a couple of steps and all of a sudden, I was on the floor on my hands and knees. I got up - a little shocked, knees slightly hurting - but said a prayer over them and kept it moving.

I could not help but to think about it - one minute I was taking steps, then literally on the floor in the next moment. I didn't even get the chance to experience the fall - that's how fast it happened. I thought to myself, "Well I got to the bottom of the stairs faster, but I would have rather taken the extra couple of steps and got there without the pain and the fall."

Over that next week, the Lord begin emphasizing to me the importance of carefully considering my steps. That it was essential that I did not skip ahead and end up missing important steps (as I literally did). God impressed upon me that in all my plans and work that I was looking to accomplish, I needed to take it step-by-step.

You won't always know what step to take - and that's where faith comes in - having faith in God because He does know. Proverbs 20:24 says, "The Lord directs our steps, so why try to understand everything along the way?" (NLT) "The Lord directs the steps of the godly. He delights in every detail of their lives." Psalms

Faith + Works is Alive

37:23 (NLT) Even if we do not know every step in advance, we can still be intentional with what the Lord has already shown us. 1 Corinthians 9:26 says, "I run with purpose with every step." (NLT) As you believe God, for whatever it is, take steps - and as you take steps, believe that God has already ordered them!

Prayer

Dear Lord I pray that where I am lacking in faith that you help my unbelief. Help me to see the way that you see, beyond my physical surroundings and with a deeper level of spiritual understanding. Faith comes by hearing Your Word, so as I read Your Word more - I know you will speak to me, hear me when I ask questions, and provide me with the steps I need to take, so that I can do your good and perfect will and experience the life that I truly want to have in You. It is in the Name of Jesus that I pray, Amen.

Chapter 9: Entrusting God with Work

Our relationship with God is the GREATEST connection that you will ever have when it comes to work. I am sure that you have heard the saying that "it's all about who you know," and that statement couldn't be truer. During my life there have been times when I would "name drop." I would mention people I knew because I believed my association to them gave me some level of validation or authenticity. Perhaps I was right in my thinking to an extent, but whose name and what relationship will ever be greater than the one we have with God? Who has more reach, pull, influence, and ability than the God Who created all people, things, and opportunities you could ever hope to attain? Nobody does or ever will, which is why He is worthy to be entrusted with this very important area of our lives.

Why should you trust God with work?

God is sovereign

God knows the outcome already and He is all-powerful. In Isaiah 7, the king and the people were afraid of what was coming against them and did not feel confident of the odds of making it out alive. God told them that what they feared, "will not happen," and to stand firm in faith because He would cause the enemies to be defeated.

"If God be for us, who can be against us?" Romans 8:30 (KJV) *No one* and *nothing!* Trust that He has gone ahead of you and that His goodness and mercy are following close behind you (Psalms 23:6), so you are covered on all sides.

God is trustworthy

Has God shown up for you in a wonderful way, when all hope seemed lost? Do not be like His children who, "forgot His [incredible works And His miraculous wonders that He had shown them." Psalms 78:11 (AMP) The same God who came through before and protected you before is still reliable and will come through again and again.

God's work is exciting

"For the Lord will rise up as at Mount Perazim, He will be stirred up as in the Valley of Gibeon, To do His Work, His unusual and incredible work, And to accomplish His work, His extraordinary work." Isaiah 28:21 (AMP) When you are working with God, He is always doing something special - there is never a dull moment walking by faith with Him.

God takes us to new levels

I have worked in a number of corporate positions. In order to get a promotion, there are usually a bunch of performance objectives you have to achieve, people you have to win the approval of, and in some cases, open spots that have to become available. However, you *Do Not* have to do all these things to be promoted and go to new heights. Yes, you who have decided to enlist God to be on your work team. How do you get promoted? "Humble yourselves, therefore, under God's mighty hand, that he may lift you up in due time. Cast all your anxiety on him because he cares for you." 1 Peter 5:6-7 (NIV) If you are looking to go deeper in God's Word on this subject, Daniel's life provides the perfect case study for how God promotes us to higher positions in our work lives. (Refer to Daniel Chapters 1, 2, 3 and 6)

You have constant Help

By believing in God and His Son, we have the Holy Spirit living within us to help us in our walk. What kind of help does the Holy Spirit provide? According to the Word He comforts us, guides us, counsels us, prays on behalf of our needs, and leads us into all truth. God is a collaborator at the highest level and in Him we have the ultimate Team that is at work with and for us.

God's Holy Spirit lives within those who have received God's free gift of salvation through Jesus Christ, God sends His angels to minister to and protect us, and Jesus Christ Himself is sitting on His heavenly throne praying on our behalf - with firsthand knowledge of every struggle we face on this earth. God is always with you and so is His Help.

Your load is light

God has already done all the heavy lifting when it comes to our work. His Word says to take His yoke upon us for His yoke is easy and His burden is light (Matthew 11:30). This essentially means that if we give all our cares about work to God daily - telling Him about those issues that we face, areas of concern, seemingly hard tasks, etc. - then He will lighten the load that we are facing and help us to overcome and accomplish what we need.

Have you ever worked for someone who felt the need to micromanage you? They assign you a task and give you the responsibility - only to then proceed to excessively supervise and interject themselves into the work that has been entrusted to you. Well, that is essentially what we do to God when we go before Him and ask for help, but then out of anxiety, fear, worry, or doubt, take back control over those tasks. Proverbs 16:3 says, "Commit your works to the

Lord [submit and trust them to Him], And your plans will succeed [if you respond to His will and guidance].

Now am I saying that you should sit around doing no work? Absolutely not! What surrendered work looks like is action, with trust attached to it, and constant communication with God throughout the day, so that you are operating in His wisdom and guidance. "To this end I labor, struggling with all His energy, which so powerfully works in me." Colossians 1:29 (NIV) You don't even have to use your own energy!

God is always available

In John 5:17, "Jesus said to them, 'My Father is always at his work to this very day, and I, too am working." (NIV) Be at peace that God is always on the clock - the Word says that He who helps us NEVER slumbers nor sleeps! So, we have God working with and for us 24/7, 7 days a week. It really doesn't get any better than that and it never will!

God is The Creator

God is not only the Creator of the universe, but He created you and can help you produce anything that He is calling you to create. When we open our bibles, the very first thing that we read about in the Word of God is how He created the earth. There is much that we began to learn and understand about God - and that includes how He took nothing and made it into something and continues to build off that something. What was the end result - it was good, it was very good: you were good, very good to Him. The work that He has started in your life is very good as well. Then after He created, He rested in the good work that He produced.

<u>Actions You Can Start Now</u>

Observe a Sabbath

God took a day to rest after six days of creation and instructed His chosen people to do the same. Jesus Himself said that "The Sabbath was made for man, not man for the Sabbath," meaning that God created a day of rest for our benefit. Mark 2:27 (NIV) A sabbath is a day that you do no work and keep holy by your actions.

So what does a day of rest look like? I used to think that you couldn't do *anything* on the Sabbath. Well Jesus said you can do good on the Sabbath, so there's nothing wrong with doing activities that are good and beneficial. I used to also think that a day of rest meant a day of sleeping. While sleep may be a part of your Sabbath, rest and sleep are not the same. The bible says that God rested on the seventh day, it also states that God never slumbers nor sleeps, so the two are not the same.

You should use that day to appreciate everything that has been done. You can trust that things won't fall apart if you take one day off because you are not the one holding things together anyways. "For anyone who enters God's rest also rests from their works, just as God did from his. Let us, therefore, make every effort to enter that rest, so that no one will perish by following their example of disobedience." Hebrews 4:10-11 (NIV)

Sin No More

I had to include this final action because throughout Jesus' ministry, after He healed someone or restored them into fellowship with God, He would tell them to, "sin no more." No this doesn't mean that we won't have moments where we slip up and yes we have God's great grace as believers in Christ, but we don't use it as an excuse to sin or treat sin nonchalantly. The Bible says over and over again that those who love God, obey God. So we obey God, not out of ritual or because He makes us, but out of Love. And luckily, we don't obey in our own strength but in His. If you are doing wrong in any area of your life, and God has told you to stop, then obey Him. If you trust Him completely, that means you trust that what He is telling you to do or not do *is for a good a reason*.

"How joyful are those who fear the Lord - all who follow his ways! You will enjoy the fruit of your labor. How joyful and prosperous you will be!" Psalms 128:1-2 (NLT)

Conclusion

Work Freedom means having a mentality about work that is completely surrendered to God. God calls us all to do different things - we are equipped with a number of skills, talents, and abilities. How do we know what to do with these God-given traits? We must give them back to the One Who gave them to us in the first place. Surrender means to cease resistance and submit to authority; hand over; abandon oneself entirely to; give in to. When I think about the most freeing and liberating action that I can take in my work journey, it is completely letting go of my own personal mindset, agenda, and attitudes about work and giving it over to God.

Simple enough, right? Perhaps not. Unfortunately, we live in a society where giving in and acquiescing seems like defeat, and maybe in certain situations it is, but you can never be defeated when placing anything in God's hands - that includes your work.

I will be honest with you. Now that you have this newfound freedom in work and in life, distractions will try to come in the form of situations, people, and opportunities to throw you off course. This is why it is extremely important to stay connected to God daily. You do not want to be ignorant of the enemy's schemes and devices.

If you keep your eyes focused on God - His Love, His Guidance, His Goodness, His Grace, His Mercy, His Peace, His Strength, His Help, and His Way - then no matter what you face, you will face it with the wisdom of God and be equipped to hold steadfast to your peace and freedom that you have found in this important area of your life. And in those moments when you start getting anxious or find yourself taking back on things that you should give over to God - be honest with yourself and God, then recommit those areas back to Him. We do not have to ever

Conclusion

be burdened by work - we can always allow God to use work as a source of provision and means for us to be a light and a reflection of Christ to others. The bible says that God cares about every detail of our lives and work is no exception!

REFUSE TO BE BOUND AGAIN

By the enemy...

By others...

and By your own self!

"So if *the Son sets* you *free*, you are truly *free*." John 8:36 (NLT)

About the Author

Brittany Ezell is an author, humanitarian, and entrepreneur. Over the past decade, Brittany has helped employees adapt to and embrace changes across their organizations as a change management and startup consultant. She is also a Change Agent for the Kingdom of God - communicating God's heart for His people and inspiring them to make positive changes.

Brittany co-leads a weekly bible study and considers it a blessing to share life experiences, dissect the Word of God, and encourage others in their faith walk. Brittany also runs a nonprofit organization, Godly Startups, where she prays over business endeavors that God has called people to and sows into work that advances the Kingdom of God.

She is a graduate of Spelman College and currently resides in Atlanta, Georgia.

Brittany would love to hear about how you have started walking in Work Freedom - share your testimony and connect with her:
www.brittanytheauthor.com

Made in the USA
Columbia, SC
21 February 2023